MW00890031

This Book Belongs To ...

....

....

....

....

Made in the USA
Monee, IL
04 December 2021

83912920R00057